BARRY FLANAGAN

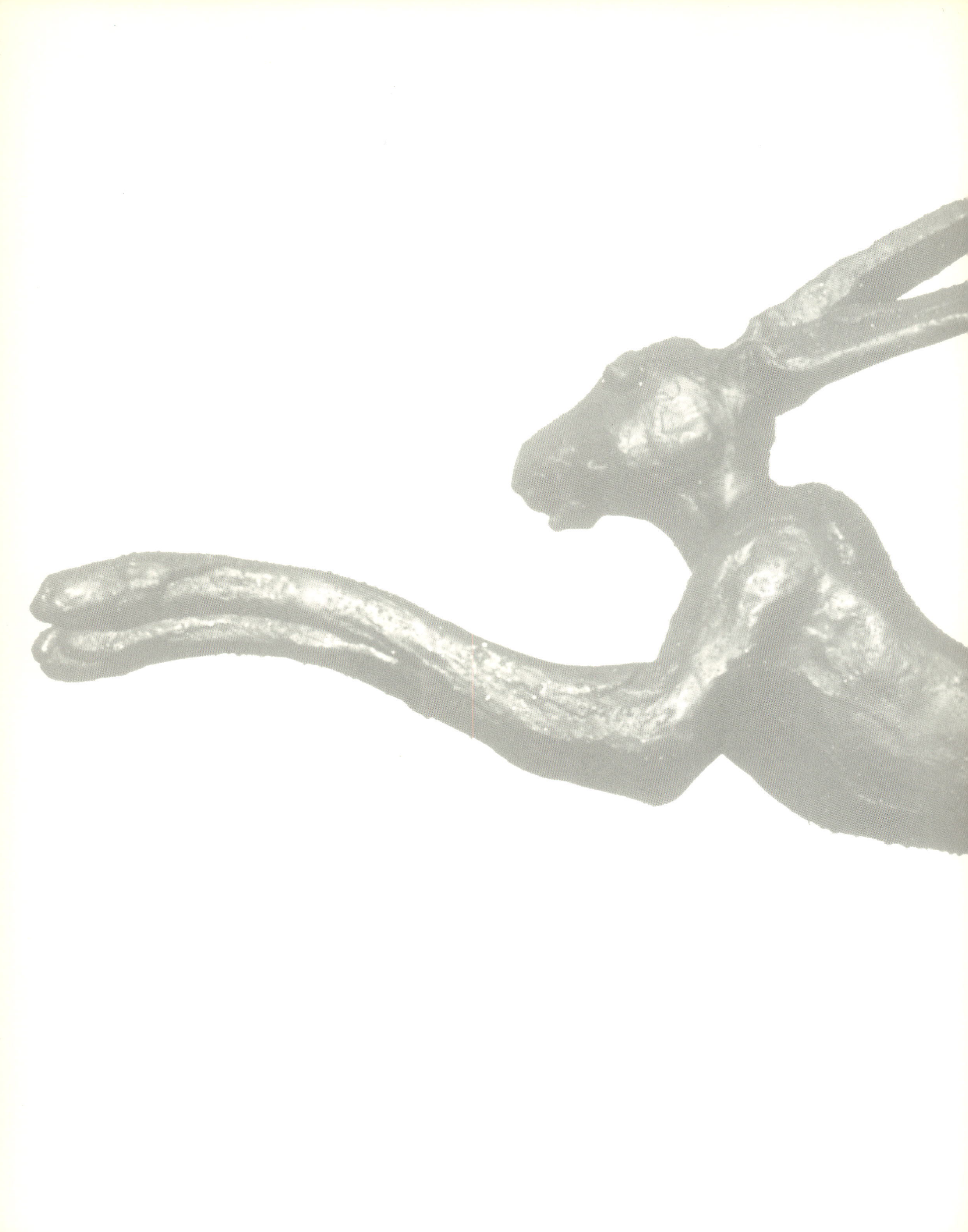

BARRY FLANAGAN

recent sculpture

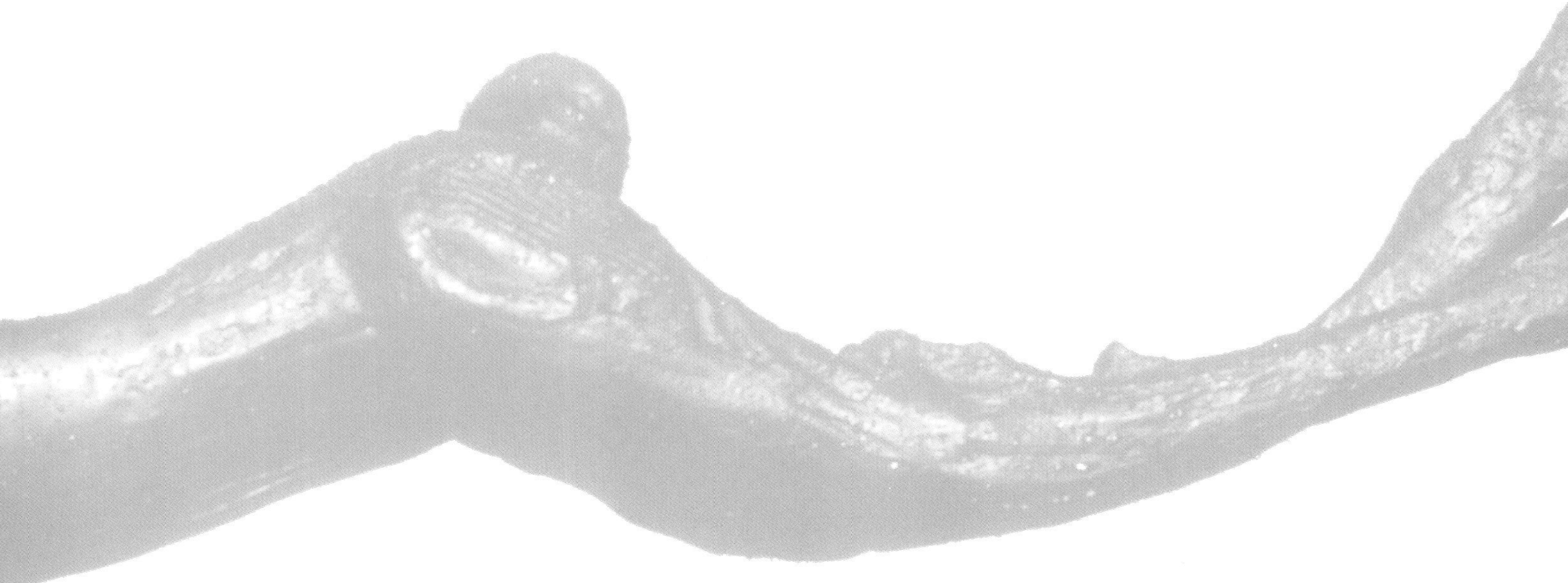

April 29 - June 30, 1994

THE PACE GALLERY 32 EAST 57 STREET NEW YORK CITY

PaceWildenstein

Thematically the choice of the hare is really quite a rich and expressive sort of model;... the investment of human attributes into the animal world is a very well practised device, in literature and film etcetera and is really quite poignant. And on a practical level, if you consider what conveys situation and meaning and feeling in a human figure, the range of expression is in fact far more limited than the device of investing an animal—a hare especially—with the expressive attributes of a human being. The ears, for instance, are really able to convey far more than a squint in an eye of a figure, or a grimace on the face of a model.

Barry Flanagan
Interview with Judith Bumpus

Bumpus, Judith. "An Interview with Barry Flanagan". *Barry Flanagan: Prints 1970-1983*, Tate Gallery, 1986.

"...In 1980, [Barry] Flanagan turned his attention to working in bronze... It is tempting to suggest... that in bronze Flanagan had at last found a material which was capable of answering many of the complex questions which had exercised him in the different phases of his previous work. Here was a material which could carry the imprint of the artist as one who acts directly to transform the material nature of things. Here was a material that could perform the complex task of representation without surrendering up its own proper nature. Here was a material which could declare the unitary nature of the sculpted object—its autonomy—unequivocally, underpinned by the authority of a traditional craft... The "Hares" spelt the beginning of a completely new phase in the artist's work, one that continues to the present. Since 1980 Flanagan has been committed to representational work, but all the while testing its limits and his own capacity to re-invent figurative tropes and traditional rhetorical forms."

Thompson, Jon. "Barry Flanagan: Artisan of Unreason". *Barry Flanagan*. Madrid, Fundación "la Caixa": 1993.

Six foot leaping hare on steel pyramid, 1990
bronze and steel, 94 x 74 x 20″
edition of 8

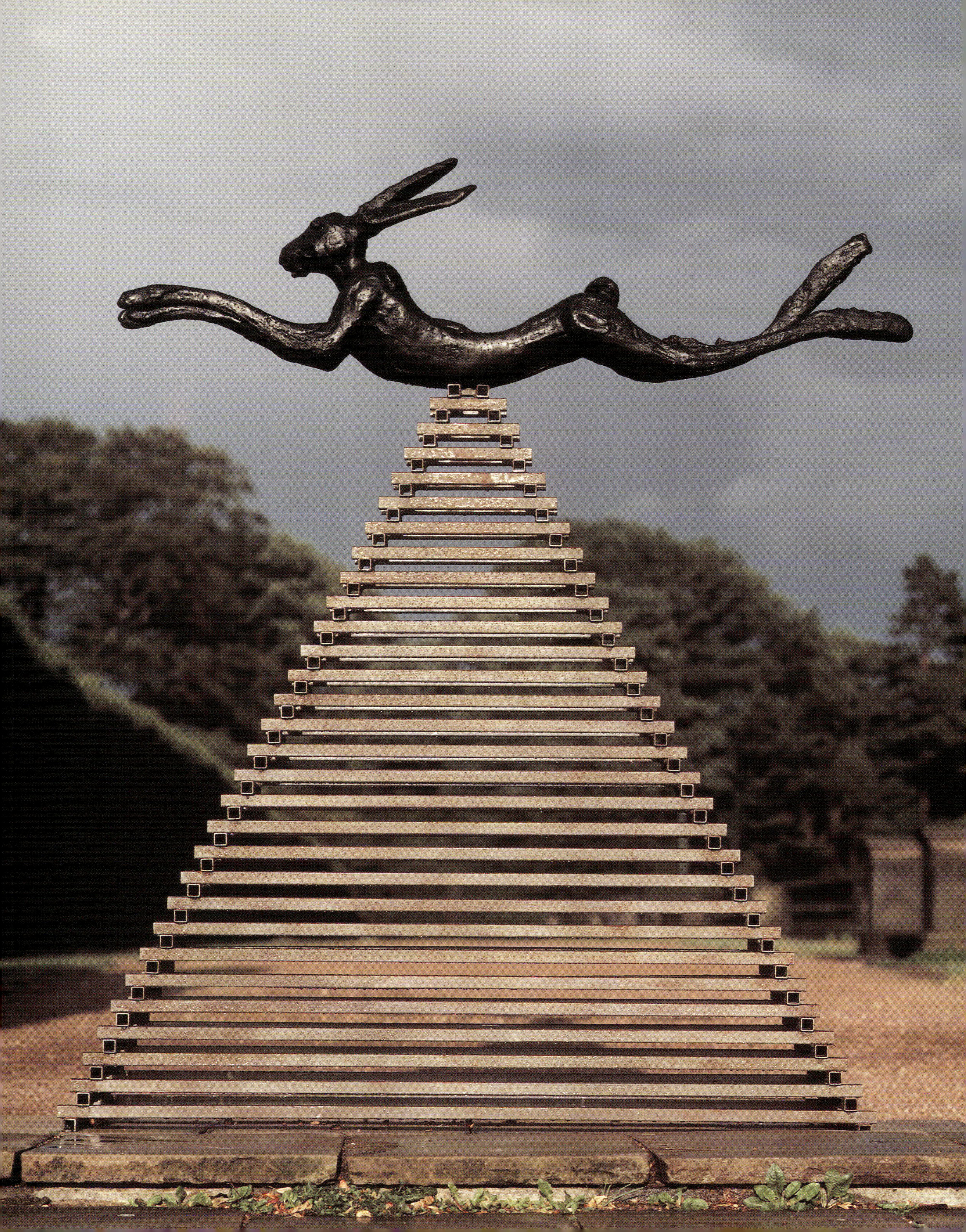

Untitled (Dancing Hare), 1989
bronze, 16½ x 7¼ x 7½"
edition of 12

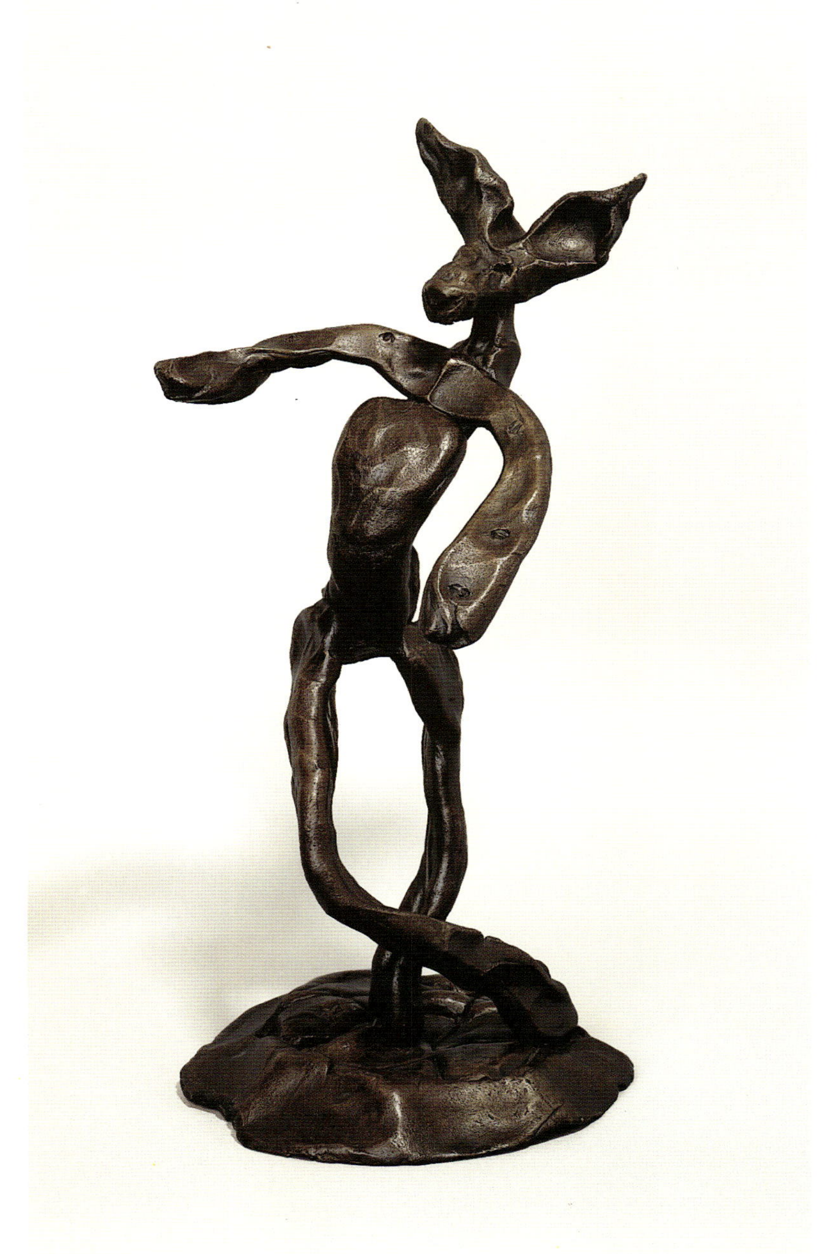

Hospitality, 1990
bronze, 118 x 183 x 66¼"
edition of 5

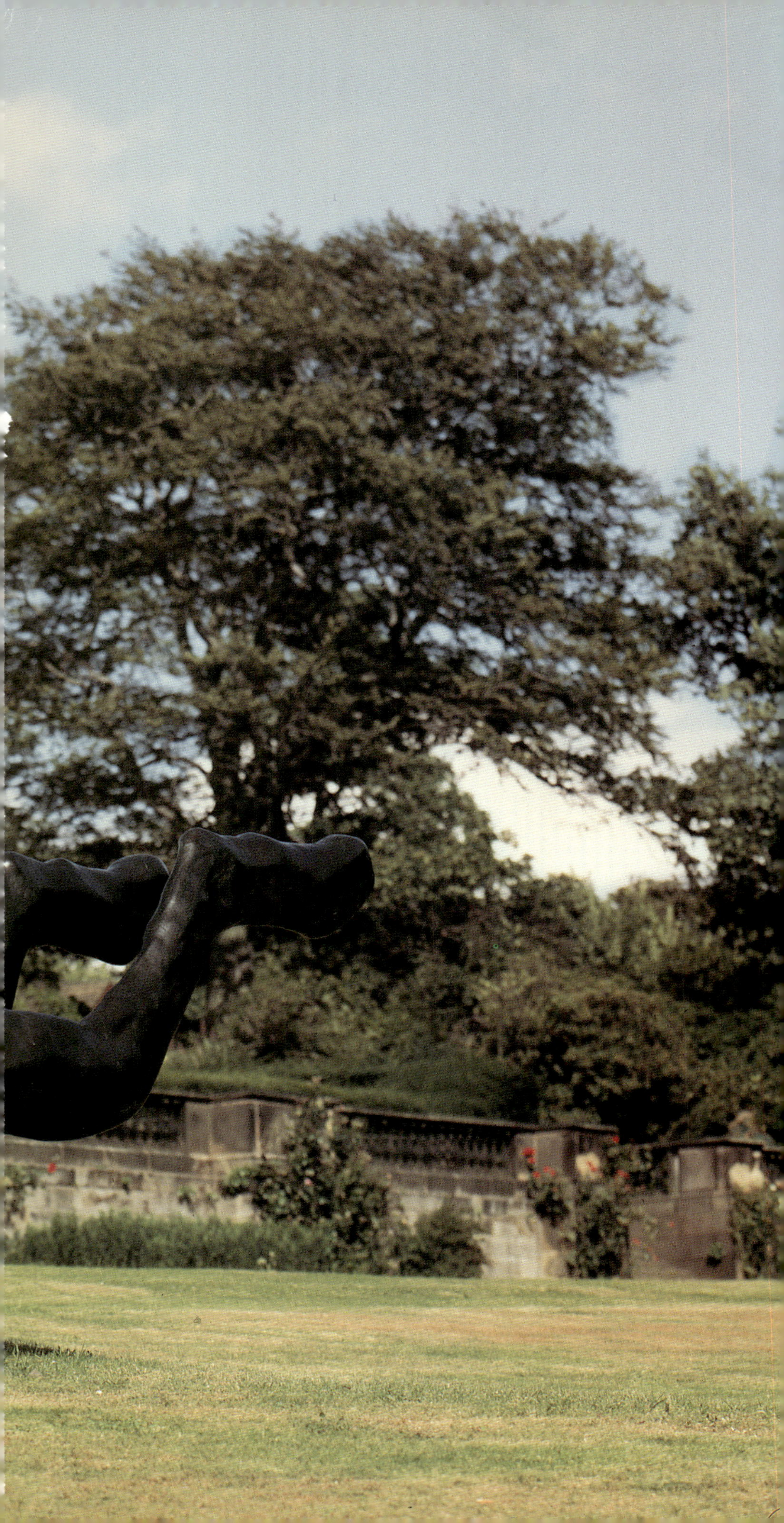

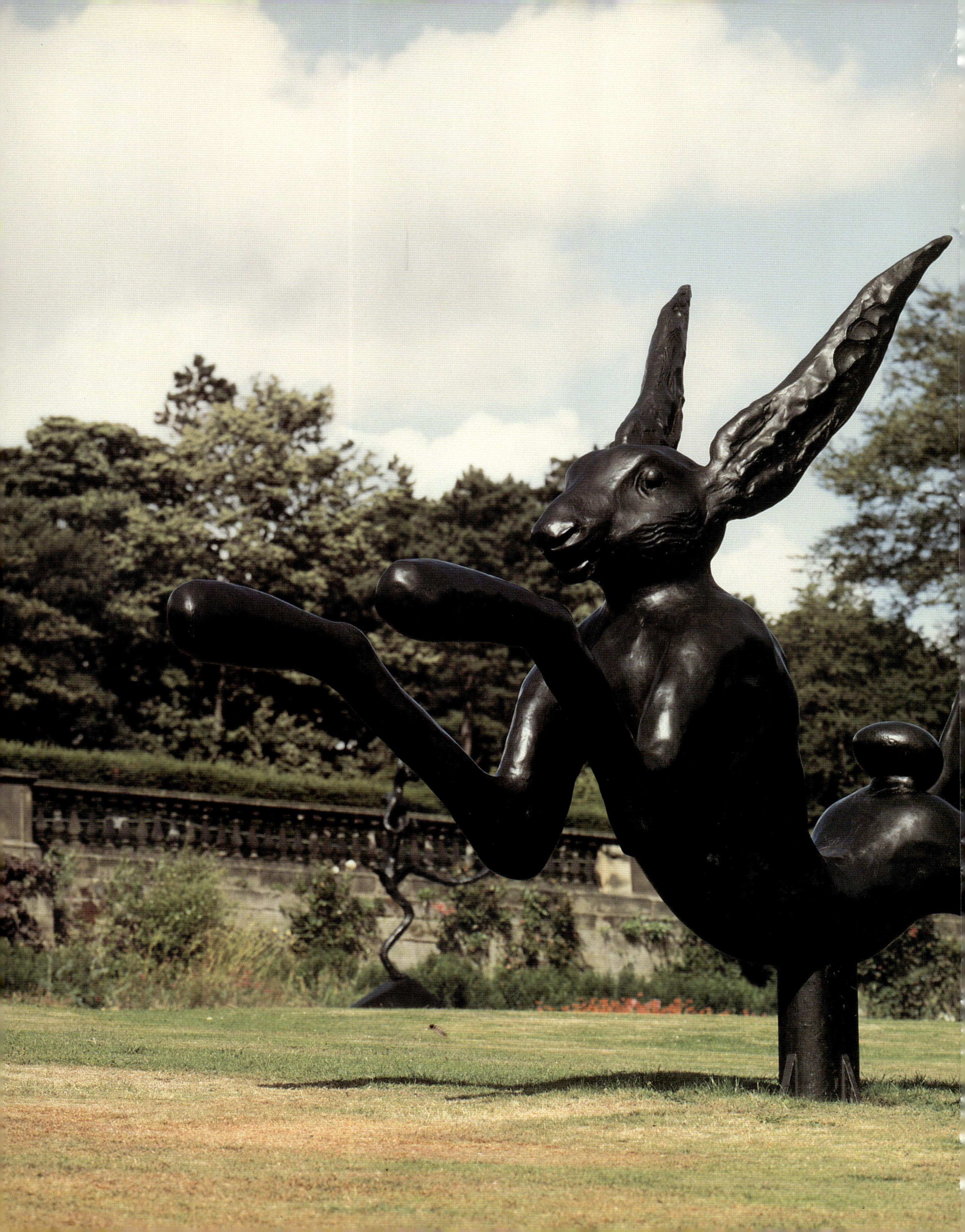

The Bowler, 1990
bronze, 120 x 33½ x 88″
edition of 8

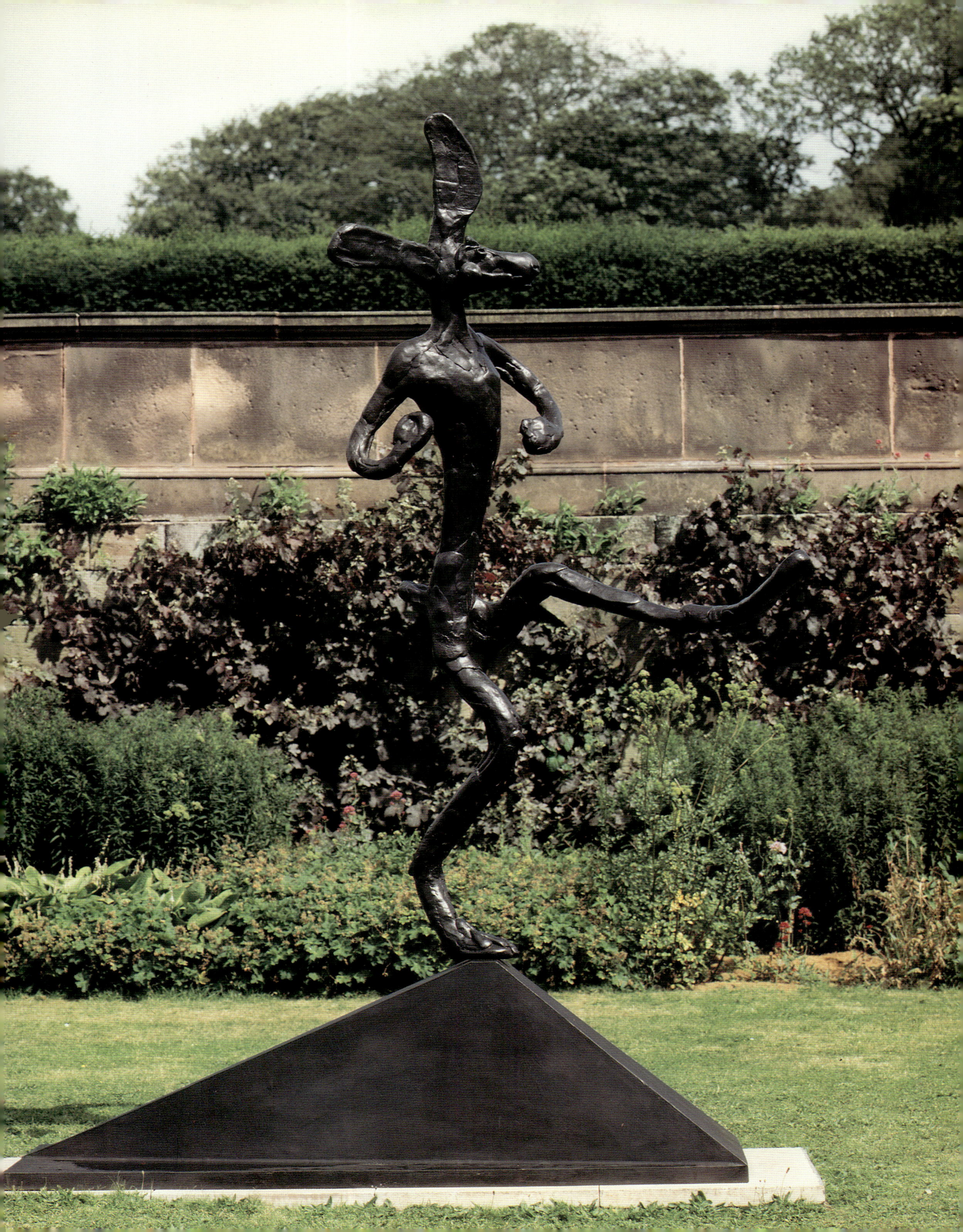

Large Mirror Nijinski, 1992
bronze, 121¾ x 89 x 36″
edition of 7

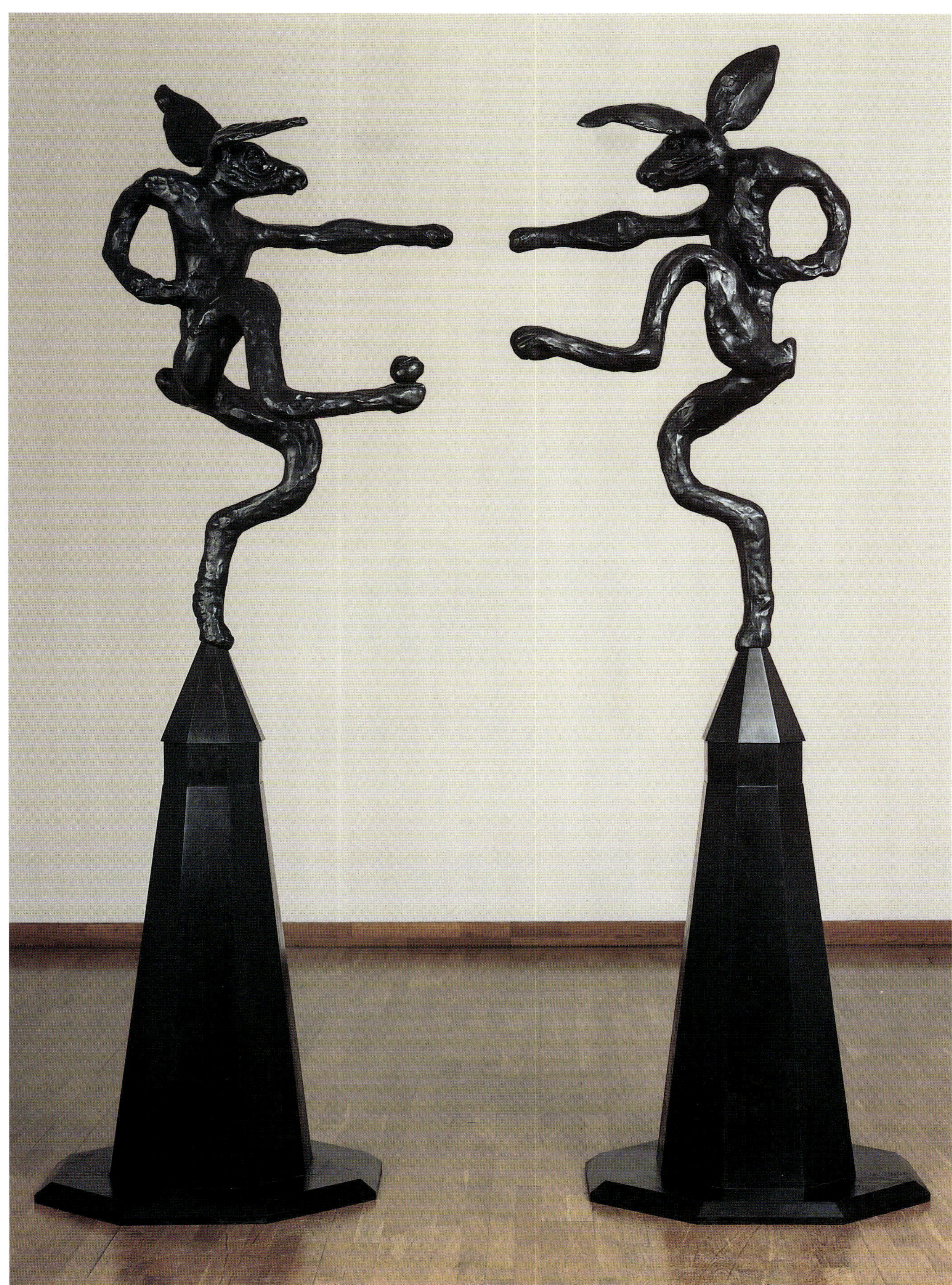

Awe, 1993
bronze, 51⅝ x 21⅝ x 15″
edition of 8

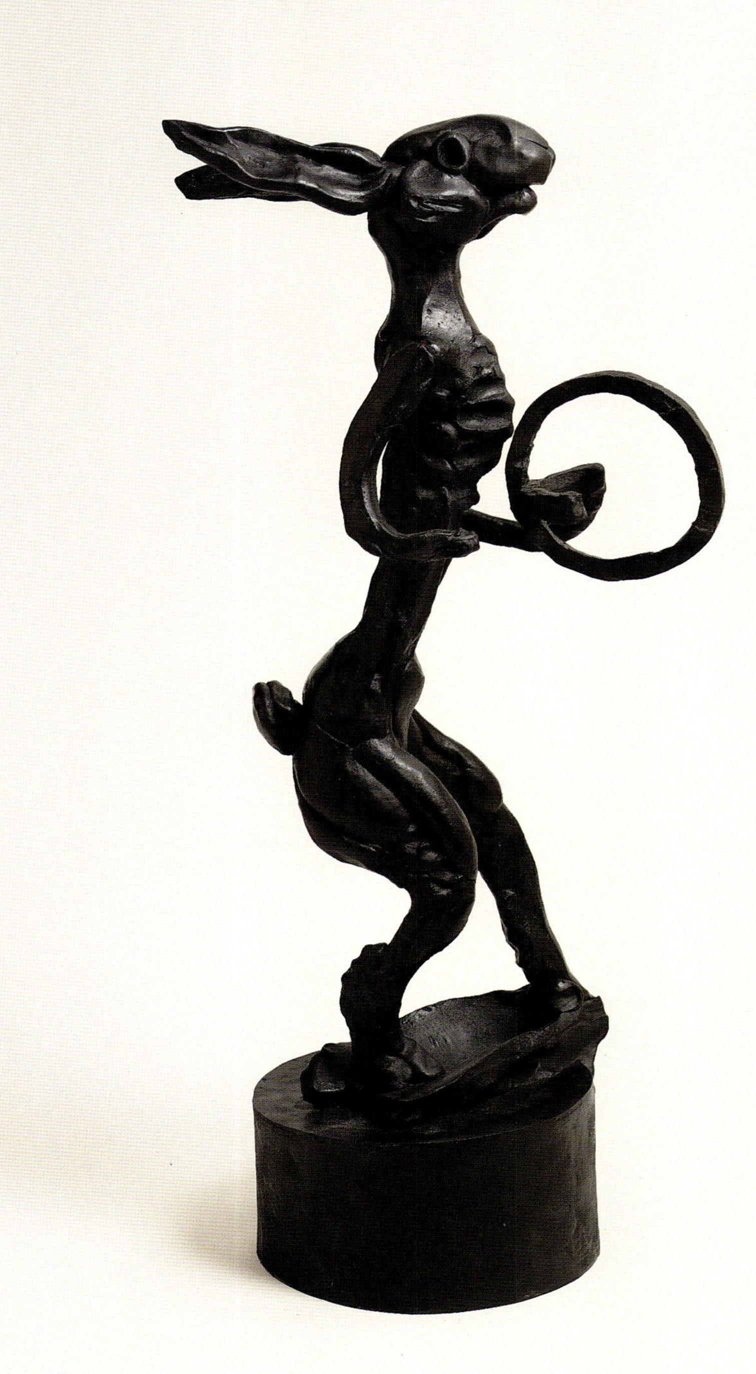

Virtue, 1993
bronze, 59⅞ x 19¾ x 15″
edition of 8

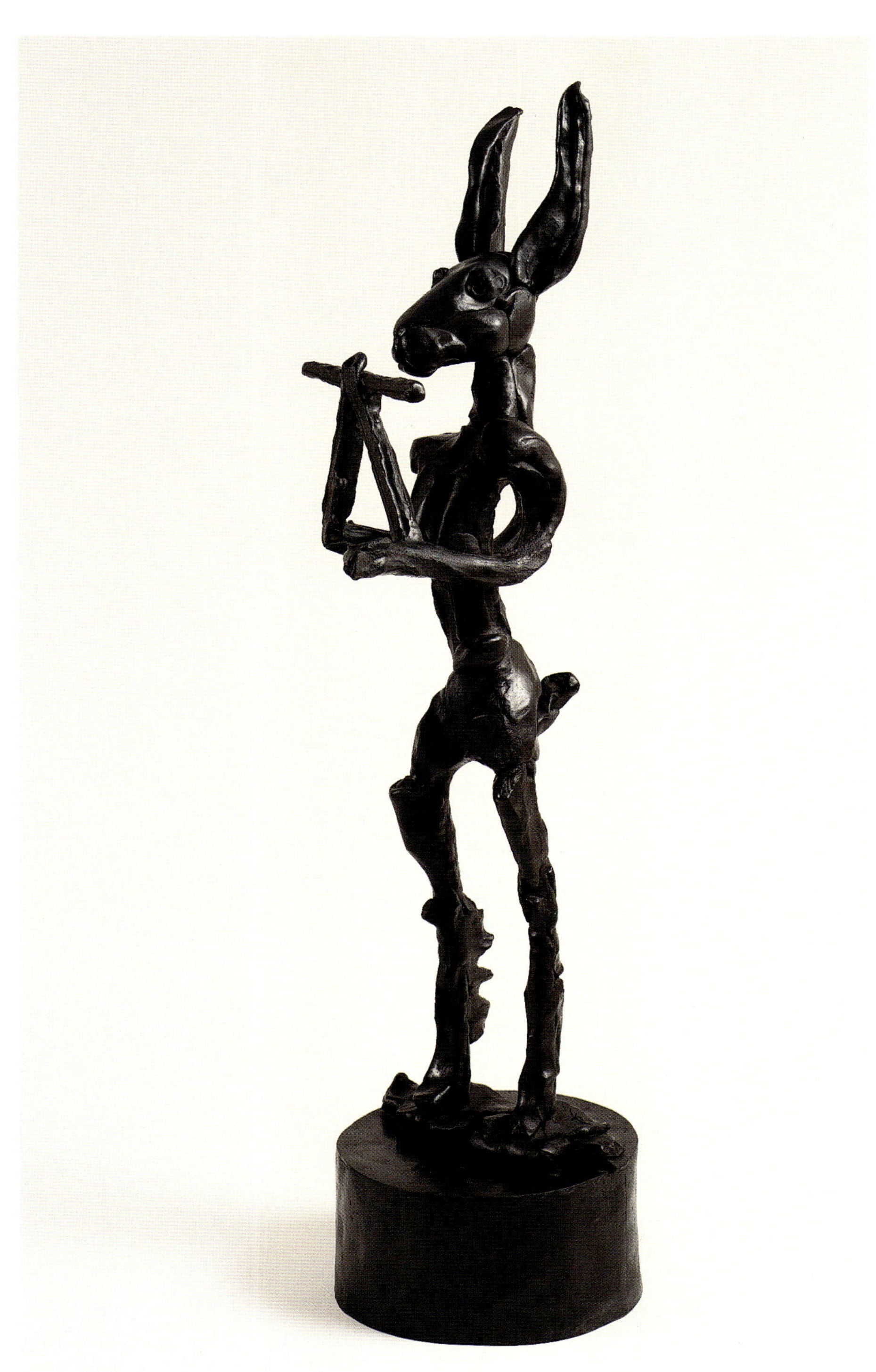

Sketch for Figure, 1993
bronze, 23⅜ x 8 x 6⅝″
edition of 8

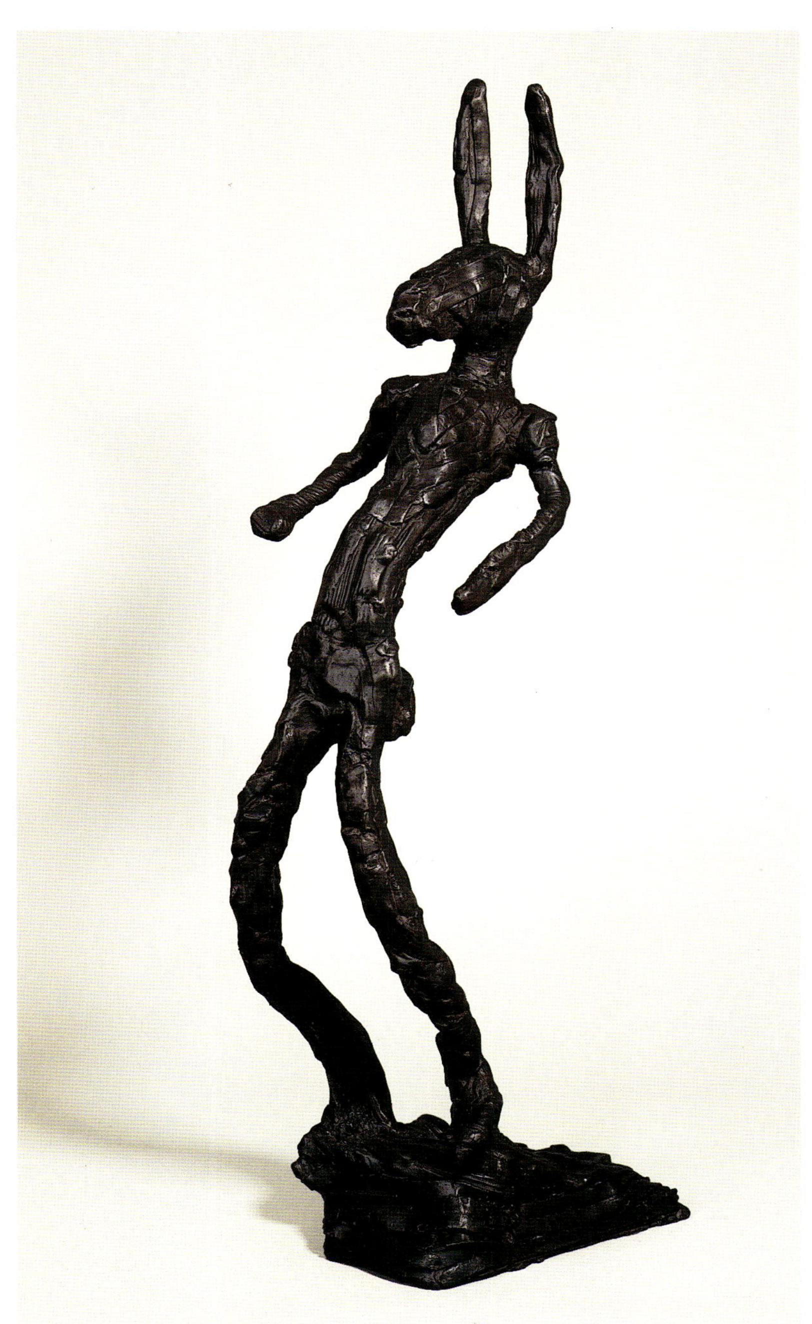

Hare with Ball, 1994
bronze, 46½ x 18¼ x 19⅜"
edition of 8

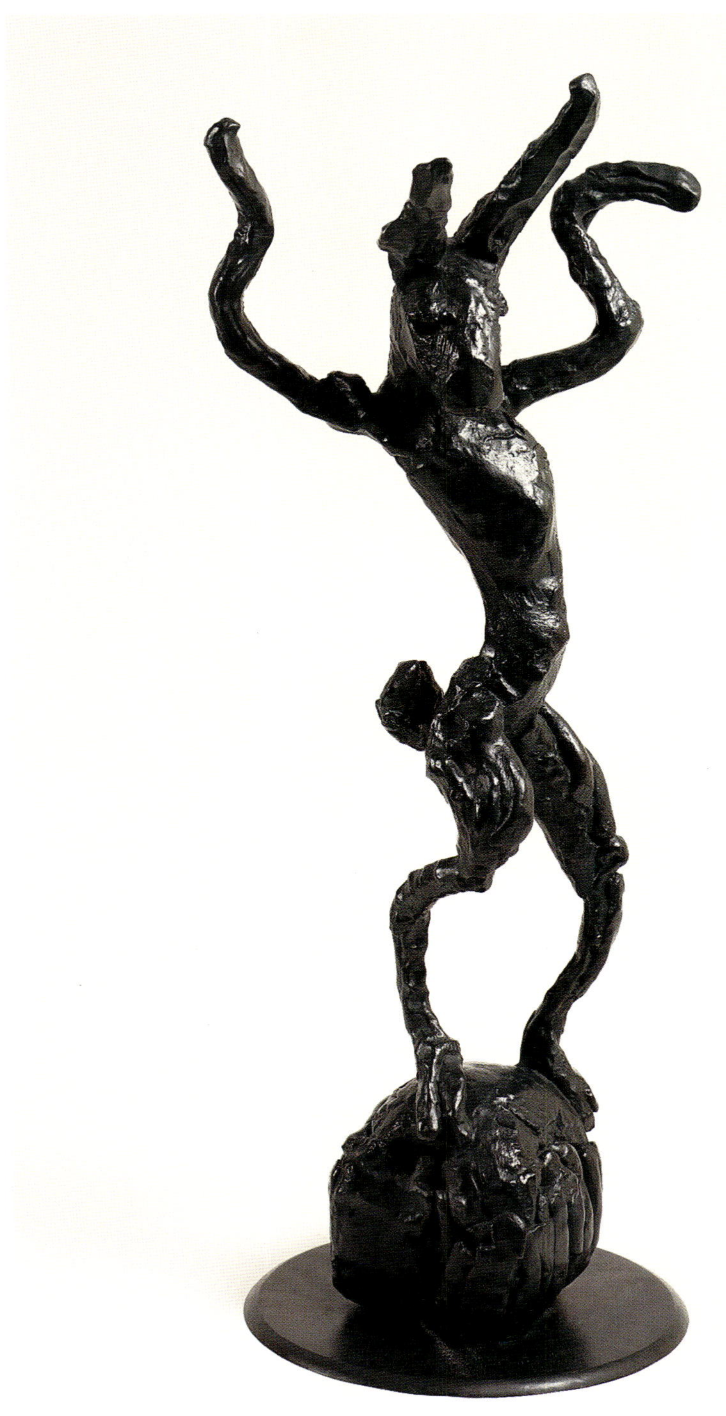

7. **Six foot leaping hare on steel pyramid**, 1990, bronze and steel, 94 x 74 x 20″, edition of 8

9. **Untitled (Dancing Hare)**, 1989, bronze, 16½ x 7¼ x 7½″, edition of 12

11. **Hospitality**, 1990, bronze, 118 x 183 x 66¼″, edition of 5

13. **The Bowler**, 1990, bronze, 120 x 33½ x 88″, edition of 8

15. **Large Mirror Nijinski**, 1992, bronze, 121¾ x 89 x 36″, edition of 7

17. **Awe**, 1993, bronze, 51⅝ x 21⅝ x 15″, edition of 8

19. **Virtue**, 1993, bronze, 59⅞ x 19¾ x 15″, edition of 8

21. **Sketch for Figure**, 1993, bronze, 23⅜ x 8 x 6⅝″, edition of 8

23. **Hare with Ball**, 1994, bronze, 46½ x 18¼ x 19⅜″, edition of 8

1941 Born January 11 in Prestatyn, Flintshire, North Wales.

1957-58 Studies architecture, sculpture, and drawing at Birmingham College of Art and Crafts, Birmingham, England.

1964-66 Studies at St. Martin's School of Art, London; receives Vocational Diploma in Sculpture with honors.

1966 First solo exhibition at Rowan Gallery, London.

1967 Teaches at Central School of Art and Crafts, London.

1969 First visit to New York for solo exhibition at Fischbach Gallery.

1970 First etchings produced at St. Martin's School of Art.

1972 Receives Gulbenkian Foundation grant to work with the dance group *Strider* in London; choreographs two small pieces.

1974 Tutored by the potter Ann Stokes.

1975 Leaves London for Northhamptonshire.

1976 Becomes associated with Waddington and Tooth Galleries, London. Returns to London.

1977 Retrospective exhibition at Stedelijk Van Abbemuseum, Eindhoven, Netherlands.

1979 Casts first *Leaping Hare*.

1980 Commissioned by the city of Ghent to produce outdoor sculpture for Sint Pietersplein. Sculpture *Camdonian* commissioned by Camden Borough Council for Lincoln's Inn Fields, London.

1983 First solo exhibition at The Pace Gallery, New York.

1984 Two bronze sculptures, *Young Elephant* and *Hare on Bell* installed at Equitable Life Tower West, New York. *Nine Foot Hare* bronze sculpture installed in atrium of Victoria Plaza, London.

1985 Helps judge Bath Sculpture Competition.

1986 Bronze sculpture *The Boxing Ones* installed at Capability Green, Luton Hoo Estate, Bedfordshire.

1987 Moves to Ibiza, Spain. Elected Associate of the Royal Academy of Arts, London. Bronze sculpture *Kouros Horse* (now known as *Field Day I*) commissioned by Hasbro Bradley, Stockley Park, Uxbridge.

1988 *Leaping Hare on a Crescent and Bell* installed at The Broadgate Centre, London.

1989 *Vizitor* commissioned for Les Halles, Paris.

1990 Two bronze *Leaping Hare* sculptures commissioned by Kawakyo Company, Osaka for the main entrance to a hotel on the Japanese coast.

1993 Major solo exhibition presented at Fundación "la Caixa", Madrid; traveling to Musée des Beaux-Arts de Nantes.

SOLO EXHIBITIONS

1966   Rowan Gallery, London

1968   Rowan Gallery, London
Barry Flanagan: Environment Skulpturen, Galerie Ricke, Kassel
Galleria dell'Ariete, Milan
Galleria Christian Stein, Turin

1969   *Barry Flanagan: Object Sculpture*, Museum Haus Lange, Krefeld
Fischbach Gallery, New York

1970   *Barry Flanagan: Recent Work*, Rowan Gallery, London

1971   Rowan Gallery, London
Galleria del Leone, Venice

1972   *Homework*, Rowan Gallery, London

1973   Rowan Gallery, London

1974   *Projects: Barry Flanagan*, The Museum of Modern Art, New York
Barry Flanagan: Exhibition of Small Works, Bluecoat Gallery, Liverpool
Barry Flanagan - Drawing 1966-1974, Museum of Modern Art, Oxford
Somethings Etruscan, Rowan Gallery, London
Drawings, Galleria dell'Ariete, Milan

1975   Hogarth Galleries, Sydney
Coil, Pinch and Squeeze Pots, Art & Project, Amsterdam

1976   Hester van Royen Gallery, London
Centro de Arte y Comunicación, Buenos Aires
(from The Museum of Modern Art, New York)

1977   *Barry Flanagan: Sculpture 1966-1976*, Stedelijk Van Abbemuseum, Eindhoven;
travels in part to Arnolfini Gallery, Bristol
Light Pieces, Art & Project, Amsterdam

1977-78   *Ceramics*, Hester van Royen Gallery, London
Graphics, Apeldoorn Museum, Netherlands

1978-79   *Barry Flanagan: Sculpture 1965-1978*, Serpentine Gallery, London

1979   *Curl Snoots*, Art & Project, Amsterdam

1980   Galerie Liliane & Michel Durand-Dessert, Paris
Sculptures in Stone 1973-1979, Waddington Galleries, London
Galerie Liliane & Michel Durand-Dessert, Paris
New 57 Gallery, Edinburgh

1981 *Sculptures in Bronze 1980-1981*, Waddington Galleries, London

1981-82 *Sixties and Seventies, Prints and Drawings by Barry Flanagan*, Mostyn Art Gallery, Llandudno, Wales; travels to Southampton Art Gallery; Institute of Contemporary Arts, London

1982-83 *Barry Flanagan Sculpture*, Biennale di Venezia, British Pavilion; travels to Museum Haus Esters, Krefeld; Galerie Liliane & Michel Durand-Dessert, Paris; Whitechapel Art Gallery, London

1983 Waddington Galleries, London

Whitechapel Art Gallery, London

Barry Flanagan Sculptures, Musée National d'Art Moderne, Centre Georges Pompidou, Paris

The Pace Gallery, New York

Centro d'Arte Contemporanea, Syracuse; travels to Certosa di San Giacomo, Capri (prints and drawings)

1984 Galerie Karsten Greve, Cologne

Waddington Graphics, London

1985 Richard Gray Gallery, Chicago

Waddington Galleries, London

Fuji Television Gallery, Tokyo

1986 Tate Gallery, London

1987-88 *Barry Flanagan, A Visual Invitation, Sculpture 1967-1987*, Laing Art Gallery, Newcastle upon Tyne; travels to Museum of Contemporary Art, Belgrade; City Gallery, Zagreb; Museum of Modern Art, Ljubljana

1988 Galerie Liliane & Michel Durand-Dessert, Paris

1990 Waddington Galleries, London

Sculptures at The Economist Plaza, London

Barry Flanagan: Sculpture, The Pace Gallery, New York

1991 *Barry Flanagan*, Fuji Television Gallery, Tokyo

1992 *Barry Flanagan*, Galerie Liliane & Michel Durand-Dessert, Paris

The Names of the Hare, Yorkshire Sculpture Park, Wakefield

Landau Fine Art, Montreal

1993-94 *Barry Flanagan*, Fundación "la Caixa", Madrid; travels to Musée des Beaux-Arts de Nantes

1994 *Barry Flanagan: Recent Sculpture*, The Pace Gallery, New York

The Art Institute of Chicago, Chicago, Illinois

Arts Council of Great Britain, London, Great Britain

The Baltimore Museum of Art, Baltimore, Maryland

British Council, London, Great Britain

Camden Borough Council for Lincoln's Inn Fields, London, Great Britain

Contemporary Art Society, London, Great Britain

Equitable Life Assurance Society, New York, New York

F.R.A.C. Rhone-Alpes, Lyon, France

Hakone Open-Air Museum, Hakone-machi, Japan

Hiroshima City Museum of Contemporary Art, Hiroshima, Japan

Israel Museum, Jerusalem, Israel

Kaiser Wilhelm Museum, Krefeld, Germany

Kunsthaus Zürich, Zurich, Switzerland

Leeds City Art Gallery, South Yorkshire, Great Britain

Leicestershire Education Authority, Leicestershire, Great Britain

Montreal Museum of Fine Arts, Montreal, Canada

Musée des Beaux Arts, Montreal, Canada

Musée des Beaux-Arts et de la Dentelle, Calais, France

Museo de Arte Contemporaneo, Caracas

The Museum of Modern Art, New York, New York

Museum of Modern Art, Wakayama, Japan

Museum van Hedendaagse Kunst, Ghent, Belgium

Nagaoka Museum, Tokyo, Japan

Nagoya City Museum, Nagoya, Japan

National Gallery of Canada, Ottawa, Canada

Peterborough Development Corporation

Phoenix Community Garden, London, Great Britain

Rawlins Upper School and Community College, Quorn, Leicestershire, Great Britain

Rijksmuseum Kröller-Müller, Otterlo, Netherlands

Roche Court Sculpture Garden, East Winterslow, Wiltshire, Great Britain

San Francisco Museum of Modern Art, San Francisco, California

Setagaya Museum, Tokyo, Japan

Sint Pietersplein, Ghent, Belgium

Southampton Art Gallery, Southhampton, Hampshire, Great Britain

Stedelijk Museum, Amsterdam, Netherlands

Stedelijk Van Abbemuseum, Eindhoven, Netherlands

Tate Gallery, London, Great Britain

Tochigi Prefectural Museum of Fine Arts, Tochigi, Japan

Tokyo Metropolitan Art Museum, Tokyo, Japan

Ulster Museum, Belfast, Northern Ireland

Victoria and Albert Museum, London, Great Britain

Virginia Museum of Fine Arts, Richmond, Virginia

Walker Art Center, Sculpture Garden, Minneapolis, Minnesota

Walker Art Gallery, Liverpool, Great Britain

Pages 2-3: detail of **Six foot leaping hare on steel pyramid**, 1990

Photography of art work:
D. James Dee, pages 17, 19 and 23
Jerry Hardman-Jones, pages 2-3, 7, 11 and 13
Richard Thomas, pages 9, 15 and 21

Catalogue designed and produced by
Tomoko Makiura and Paul Pollard for PaceWildenstein.

Library of Congress Catalog Card Number: 94-60552
ISBN: 1-878283-44-8